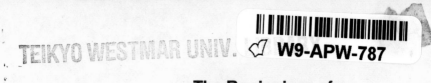

The Beginnings of
Musical Nationalism
in Brazil

Detroit Monographs in Musicology   Number 1

The Beginnings of Musical Nationalism in Brazil

Gerard Behague

91-1765

Information Coordinators, Inc.   Detroit

Cover design by Peter Nothstein

Published by
Information Coordinators, Inc.
1435-37 Randolph Street
Detroit, Michigan 48226

TABLE OF CONTENTS

FOREWORD

The present study is a revised portion of the author's doctoral thesis titled "Popular Musical Currents in the Art Music of the Early Nationalistic Period in Brazil, ca. 1870-1920." One of the purposes of that study was to define as accurately as possible the urban popular musical traditions of the period under consideration, and to determine whether the art-composers turned their attention to the vernacular because of inherent interest or whether they simply followed the concurrent European nationalistic tendency. The process of transformation of folksong and dance into urban popular forms, Brazilian in character, was examined thoroughly in the larger project of the thesis.

I wish to express my deepest gratitude and appreciation to the various persons who assisted me in a number of ways in the completion of this study, especially Professor Gilbert Chase, Mr. Sergio Nepomuceno Alvim Corrêa, Dr. Francisco Curt Lange, Dr. Luiz Heitor Corrêa de Azevedo, and Dr. Heitor Martins.

Gerard Behague

INTRODUCTION

IN THE late nineteenth and early twentieth centuries, musical nationalism became the most important motivating force in the creation of art music in Brazil. The early phase of nationalism in Brazil may be defined as a time of transition whose stylistic trends stand between early romantic European national music, as expressed in Brazil by Carlos Gomes's operas or Itiberê da Cunha's piano piece A Sertaneja, and more authentic nationalism rooted in folk and popular musical traditions. Only after 1920 was this latter aspect developed by such composers as Villa-Lobos, Mignone, Lorenzo Fernandez, and Guarnieri.

The composers of this transitional period (ca. 1880-1920) continued to be essentially academic; their ideals were geared largely to European romantic and post-romantic music, including the universal Wagnerian influence. Although their attitude toward 'genuine' Brazilian music which emerged around the same time was not negative (for Europe itself had made it fashionable to compose on folk-popular themes), the difficulty lay in their ignorance of it. The final purpose of this study is to attempt to determine to what extent these composers turned their attention to the vernacular because of its inherent interest or to what extent they simply followed the concurrent European nationalistic tendency.

By 1880 folk and ethnic music investigations in Brazil were beginning with Silvio Romero's first publications appearing in 1883. Yet even as late as 1913-1917, when Edgardo Roquette Pinto published his first studies, art-music composers remained generally unaware of these publications. Furthermore, in such cosmopolitan environments as those of Rio de Janeiro and São Paulo, where most of the composers of this period were active, folk music was scarcely known during the nineteenth century. It took at least thirty years after the proclamation of the Republic (1889) for folk music significantly to penetrate these urban areas. Therefore, during the period under consideration, there could not be any direct assimilation of folk music in Rio de Janeiro or São Paulo. Yet in the case of provincial cities, especially those in the north and northeast, folk manifestations could not be considered as a purely rural phenomenon. The critic-musicologist Mário de Andrade has stressed this interpenetration of the rural and the urban cultural areas making clear that, with the exception of Rio, São Paulo, and a few others, "all Brazilian cities are in direct and immediate contact with the rural zone."[1] This will prove particularly important in the case of the composer Alberto Nepomuceno who, in his adolescence, lived in such northeastern provincial cities.

*   *   *

1. Mário de Andrade, Ensaio sôbre a música brasileira (São Paulo: Livraria Martins Editôra, 1962) p. 166.

Amerindian tunes were available through such works as Jean de Lery's Histoire d'un voiyage en la terre du Brésil, autrement dit Amérique; Spix and Martius' Reise in Brasilien; Barbosa Rodrigues' Pacificação dos Crichanás and Poranduba Amazonense; Karl von den Steinen's Unter den Naturvölkern Zentral-Brasiliens; or Nicolas Badariotti's Exploração no Norte de Mato Grosso. But the art-music composers felt that Indian music stood too far removed from their cultural heritage to be the source of 'national' music (even the Indianist elements in some of Villa-Lobos' works remained insignificant). Since folk music was largely unfamiliar and Indian music seemed remote, it was natural that urban popular forms came to be regarded as the nearest and most obvious source of national music. Furthermore, the popularity of such forms as the 'lundu' and 'modinha', the 'maxixe', and the early 'samba' guaranteed them immediate recognition as characteristic national expressions.

To what extent these urban popular forms influenced the nationalistic compositions of the period will be seen in our study of three composers who appear as leading figures in this early phase of nationalism: Brasilio Itiberê da Cunha, Alexandre Levy, and Alberto Nepomuceno.

BRASILIO ITIBERÊ DA CUNHA
(1846-1913)

EARLY ROMANTIC musical nationalism as expressed by such composers as Chopin and Liszt had its counterpart in Brazil for the first time with the Austrian pianist-composer Sigismund Neukomm, who used a 'lundu' theme in his fantasy for piano O Amor Brasileiro (1819). An autograph of this piece was discovered by Mozart de Araújo at the Paris Conservatory Library in 1952. These variations on a popular theme do not represent, however, a point of departure for Brazilian national music, because the 'lundu'-song itself presented few national characteristics at that time, and because they follow the conventional style of all 'themes and variations' written in the early nineteenth century.

The first 'nationalist' composition was published in 1869 by an amateur musician and a remarkable pianist, Brasilio Itiberê da Cunha, "compositore di cose gentili" as Cernicchiaro describes him. [2] Itiberê da Cunha was a diplomat and an habitué of the salons of the Second Empire in Brazil, as well as those of Europe. He was born in Paranaguá, but soon moved to São Paulo where he studied for a diplomatic career. His first public appearance as a pianist occurred in 1882 at Rio de Janeiro. By this time his fame was well established in the Empire, as indicated by the following announcement in the satirical weekly magazine Revista Illustrada:

> "On Monday, July 10th, at the São Pedro d'Alcantara theatre, a grand lyric-dramatic spectacle will be presented, dignified by the august presence of Their Imperial Majesties, for the benefit of the Educational Fund. In this spectacle, organized by Mme Alina Alhaiza from the Lyric Theatre of Paris, we will hear for the first time in Rio de Janeiro, our distinguished pianist and amateur composer, the Baron Itiberê. "[3]

Itiberê da Cunha lived in Berlin for many years, as minister plenipotentiary. There he became acquainted with some of the leading composers of the time, among them Liszt, who played his works, and Anton Rubinstein, to whom he dedicated his Etude de Concert (d'après C. P. E. Bach). From Liszt he certainly learned the "rather exhibitionistic and charlatanic brilliance, " referred to by Einstein;[4] but his style -- with its

*   *   *

2. Vincenzo Cernicchiaro, Storia della Música nel Brasile dai tempi coloniali sino ai nostri giorni, 1549-1925 (Milano: Fratelli Riccioni, 1926) p. 338.
3. "Pequeno Correio, " Revista Illustrada, July 8 1882, p. 6.
4. Alfred Einstein, Music in the Romantic Era (New York: W. W. Norton & Co., 1947) p. 215.

abuse of virtuoso effects, its harmonic clichés, and its rhythmic regularity --
remained too imitative of European romantic piano music, without manifesting
a thorough assimilation of it. Such works as <u>Nuits Orientales</u>,
<u>Barcarolle Vénitienne</u>, <u>Soirées à Venise</u>, <u>Sous les
Tropiques</u>, and <u>Rhapsodies Brésiliennes</u>, presented, in addition,
a false exoticism which openly attempted to renew the success that Gottschalk
had obtained in Europe with such pieces as <u>La Savane</u>, <u>Le Bananier</u>,
and <u>La Bamboula</u>.

The name of Brasilio Itiberê would probably have been forgotten were
it not for the piano piece <u>A Sertaneja</u> which recreates in various ways the
atmosphere of urban popular music, even quoting a characteristic popular
melody. He was twenty-three when he wrote this "characteristic fantasy,"
Opus 15, considered by many as a "starting point" of Brazilian national music.
Eighteen hundred sixty nine was the year of Gottschalk's triumphs in Rio de
Janeiro as well as in all the large provincial cities. The example of Gottschalk
may have deeply impressed the young Itiberê, for the practice of introducing
popular elements in art music was certainly not the tendency at this early
period. <u>A Sertaneja</u>, still frequently performed today in Brazil,
unquestionably presents national elements derived from the popular forms
such as the 'maxixe', the Brazilian 'tango', or the popular 'modinha'.

In the long introduction, passages based primarily on virtuosic display
(arpeggios alternating between A-flat major and A-flat minor) contrast with
"a sorrowful phrase characteristic of the melancholy of our race. " [sic][5]

Example 1 (m.m. 1-17)

*   *   *

5. Iwan d'Hunac [João Itiberê da Cunha], "Um precursor da música
brasileira, " <u>Illustração Musical</u>, I (1930) 1.

This leads to the first section, in the character of a scherzo, which includes a characteristic dominant pedal, and the accentuation of the weak part of the beat ♪♪♪ :

Example 2 (m.m. 27-31)

Variation of the latter figure is noticeable in the reiteration of the first theme, ♪♪♪♪ . In a contrasting spirit, the first popular motive, invented by the composer, recalls directly the sentimental character of the salon 'modinha',[6]

*   *   *

6. The 'modinha' as an art-song and salon genre has been the subject of several good studies. Cf. Mário de Andrade, <u>Modinhas Imperiais</u>. São Paulo: Casa Chiarato L. G. Miranda, 1930. Also Mozart de Araújo, <u>A Modinha e o Lundu no Século XVIII</u>. São Paulo: Ricordi Brasileira, 1963. For a study of the differences between the Portuguese and the Brazilian 'modinha', see G. Béhague "Biblioteca da Ajuda MSS 1595/1596: Two Eighteenth Century Anonymous Collections of Modinhas, " in <u>Yearbook</u>, IV, Inter-American Institute for Musical Research, 1968.

with the typical modulation to the subdominant and the appoggiaturas in
the treble:

Example 3 (m.m. 46-52)

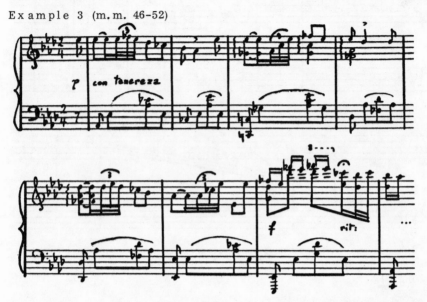

The repetition of the first section leads to the literal quotation of the traditional
tune "Balaio, meu bem, balaio," widely in vogue in the entire country at that
time. 'Balaio' was both a song and a dance related to the 'fandango'. It should
be pointed out that in Brazil the term 'fandango' lost its original Spanish
meaning around the end of the eighteenth century, and was used to designate
a social festive entertainment with dancing. [7] Thus, we find several dances
associated with the Brazilian 'fandango', among them the 'balaio'. For each
dance there was also a corresponding song whose incipit often determined
the actual name of the dance in which this song was incorporated. Although
the 'balaio' dance became more typical of the state of Rio Grande do Sul,
Augusto Meyer found ample evidence that it originated in the northeastern
provinces of Bahia and Pernambuco, from the primitive 'lundu' dance, and
was diffused all over the country. [8]

The song "Balaio, meu bem, balaio" had the basic dotted figure

*   *   *

7. Cf. Augusto Meyer, Cancioneiro Gaúcho (Rio de Janeiro: Editôra
Globo, 1952) pp. 183-4. The author verified the same acceptation in
all the Hispano-American area, including the North American states
of Texas, New Mexico, and California, in which, according to
Bartlett's Dictionary of Americanisms, "this term is applied to
a ball or dance of any sort."
8. Ibid., p. 17.

14

of almost all 'fandango' dances in Brazil, calling for repeated notes:[9]

Example 4   "Balaio, meu bem, balaio"

Itiberê da Cunha used the melody in an inner part, within a virtuoso accompaniment according to the prevailing standard of piano writing. But the superposition of the figures ♪♪♪ and ♪♪♪ with simple harmonic progressions and repetition of the same pattern throughout, makes this section come closer to the urban 'maxixe', or the Brazilian 'tango' as developed by such popular composers as Ernesto Nazareth:[10]

Example 5   (m. m. 91-7)

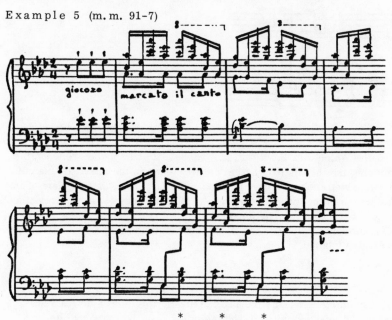

*   *   *

9. Transcribed in F. J. de Santa-Anna Nery, Le Folklore Brésilien (Paris: Perrin et Cie., 1889) p. 277.
10. The music of Ernesto Nazareth (1863-1934) has been the subject of very few good studies. Besides Brasílio Itiberê's "Ernesto Nazareth na música brasileira, " in Boletin Latino-Americano de Música, VI (Apr 1946) 311-12; we find a much better insight in Jaime C. Diniz's monograph Nazareth, estudos analíticos (Recife: Departamento de Extensão Cultural e Artística, 1963).

The next section imitates the Brazilian tango with its characteristic habanera rhythm, much in the manner of the popular composer Antonio Callado's first typical polkas, keeping the choreographic elements of the melodic line by means of neighboring tones, appoggiaturas, and passing tones:

Example 6 (m.m. 120-23)

Joaquim Antonio da Silva Callado (1848-1880) was indeed responsible for popularizing the 'habanera' rhythm as it is found in the previous example. His most celebrated 'polka' Que rida por todos was, in fact, one of the earliest examples of an authentic 'maxixe'. In it the composer very ingeniously transformed the 'habanera' rhythm 2/4 ♫♩♫ into ♪♪♪ and ♪♪♪♪ in the bass accompaniment, pointing the way to the rhythmic patterns of the later urban samba and 'chôro':[11]

*   *   *

11. Commenting on this passage, Luiz Heitor Corrêa de Azevedo wrote: "The syncopation of the melody and of the intermediate part, the long melodic impulse which goes through the eight bars without any loss of continuity, reaching its peek in the fourth bar and declining gradually with the uniform rhythm of the eighth notes -- all this is typical of the urban 'maxixe', in this completely 'de-Europeanized' piece that has nothing of the polka but the name." (In 150 Anos de Música no Brasil, 1800-1950) (Rio de Janeiro: Livraria José Olympio Editôra, 1956) p. 146.

Example 7   Callado's <u>Querida por todos</u>

    <u>A Sertaneja</u> oscillates throughout between A-flat major and its minor homonym, recalling the prevailing modulatory process of the 'modinha', of the Second Empire. [12] The historical importance of Itiberê da Cunha's piece has been overestimated. The composer himself probably regarded it as a fanciful and youthful composition of no further consequence, for Vincenzo Cernicchiaro, who knew Itiberê personally, does not mention <u>A Sertaneja</u> in his book, nor does it appear in the concert programs of the time. [13] This assumption is also confirmed by the fact that the composer did not continue in the direction of <u>A Sertaneja</u>. Although this piece has no influence on later developments of musical nationalism in Brazil, it nevertheless remains significant for having introduced popular musical elements, and for reproducing, though superficially, the atmosphere of the characteristic urban popular music.

*　　　*　　　*

12. This modulatory aspect of the 'modinha' has been studied by Mário de Andrade: "The impression given is that those composers of 'modinhas' had a sixteenth-century harmonic sensibility, conceiving the minor mode, not as another mode, but as the major mode with the third degree lowered. They used it as such to give variety to the tonal physiognomy. "
13. Cf., e.g., the program for his inaugural concert in Rio, in <u>Revista Illustrada</u>, July 8 1882, pp. 6-7.

17

ALEXANDRE LEVY
(1864-1892)

ROMANTIC MUSICAL nationalism in Brazil -- impregnated with some elements of popular music -- is best represented in its early phase by Alexandre Levy, in spite of the short duration of his career. He was the first Brazilian composer to take a definite interest in folk and popular music, and to use popular themes systematically in his most important works.

Of French descent, Levy was born in the city of São Paulo in 1864 to a family of musicians. He studied piano and composition with European professional immigrants: Gabriel Giraudon for the piano, Georg von Madeweiss and Gustav Wertheimer for harmony and composition. Around 1880 São Paulo was developing into a rather important center for music. Instrumental and vocal concerts were frequent and the organization of musical associations and clubs was taking shape. Levy was largely responsible for the foundation of the Haydn Club in 1883, sponsoring and conducting concerts of the symphonic repertoire generally unknown in São Paulo at that time. With his departure for Europe in 1887, the club ceased all activities, showing how dynamic a role he must have played in this society.[14]

Levy's sojourn in Europe was very short. After three months in Milan he stayed in Paris from June to November of 1887, studying harmony with Emile Durand at the Conservatory, and attending regularly the Colonne and Lamoureux concerts. The stimulus of these concerts was such that he wrote the Andante of his Symphony in E Minor at this time, and preferred the orchestral medium in his subsequent works.

Upon his return to São Paulo, he continued his activities as composer and conductor. Under his direction the Mendelssohn Club presented Weber's Der Freischütz for the first time in Brazil. He also attempted to organize a regular symphony orchestra in order to reveal to the public of São Paulo the repertoire he had heard in Paris. But he did not find much support, so that a few years before his death he was moved to say that the situation of music in Brazil was shameful.[15]

Levy's approach to folk and popular music was strictly sentimental. His fantasy for two pianos on O Guarany (Opus 2 1882), manifests his early admiration for Carlos Gomes and the latter's incipient nationalism. But it is significant to observe that Levy's most important nationalistic compositions were written during or after his stay in Europe. Paris,

*   *   *

14. Cf. Luiz Heitor Corrêa de Azevedo, 150 Anos..., pp. 156-7.
15. "Alexandre Levy," Gazeta Musical, II n4 (Feb 1892) 58.

18

doubtless, stimulated the cultivation of national musics at that time. Since the foundation of the National Society for French Music in 1871, the revival of French tradition within romantic moulds was carried out by such composers as Saint-Saens, Massenet, and Fauré. This together with the Russian, Czech, and Norwegian nationalist movements, may have provided a strong motivation for the young Levy. His travel companion in Paris, João Gomes Junior, recounted to the music critic Carlos Penteado de Rezende that when discussing music Levy often repeated that every nation had its characteristic music, and that Brazil would some day reveal its own. In Levy's opinion, in order to write 'Brazilian' music it was necessary to study the folk and popular music of all regions of Brazil, especially that of the northern states. [16] But the only popular forms available to him were, of course, 'modinhas' and 'lundus', which, according to Rezende, he appreciated very much. The only folk dance with which he might have come in contact in his native state was the 'samba' of São Paulo. Otherwise his knowledge of folk music remained limited to anonymous, widely spread traditional songs such as "Balaio, meu bem, balaio, " or "Vem cá, bitu. "

Levy's awareness of urban popular music, especially of Callado's pieces, is readily seen in some of his piano works, among which the most characteristic is the Tango Brazileiro. [17]

It is not known for certain whether the Variations sur un thème Brésilien were written before or after the composer's departure for Europe. In a Festschrift honoring Levy and published in the Gazeta Musical (1892), we are told a sentimental story about the circumstances of the composition. According to this, Levy, alone in Paris, wrote these variations in a homesick mood.[18] But João Gomes Junior, who met Levy immediately after his arrival in Milan, reported that the variations were performed at the Conservatory of that city for the teacher Dominicetti Giovanini. [19] Considering that the composer had the opportunity to have his works published in São Paulo because his father owned a music publishing house there, it is quite probable that he composed these variations during his trip to Europe or soon after his arrival in Milan. The fact that Levy gave French titles to this and most of his works is without significance, for he was merely following the romantic tradition that had become fashionable.

*   *   *

16. Carlos Penteado de Rezende, "Alexandre Levy na Europa em 1887, " O Estado de São Paulo, Jan 19 1946.
17. Ernesto Vieira, Diccionario Biographico de Musicos Portuguezes (Lisbon: Typographia Mattos Moreira e Pinheiro, 1900) Vol. II, pp. 31-3.
18. Gazeta Musical..., pp. 53-4.
19. Carlos Penteado de Rezende, op. cit., p. 4.

The theme used in the variations came from a popular song of the early nineteenth century, "Vem cá Bitu," one of the most celebrated traditional melodies of Brazil, still much in vogue as a children's song. According to the folklorist João Ribeiro, this song is related to a rural round dance called 'siriri' or 'ciriri' which had two versions, one from Pernambuco[20] and the other from Mato Grosso.[21] Renato Almeida asserts that he was unable to find specific indication of the choreography of the northern version of the dance.[22] The German author Max Schmidt in his Indianerstudien in Zentralbrasilien (1905) described the Mato Grosso version as a round dance. According to Ribeiro, the song itself relates only to the northern variant.

The tune displays a European melodic structure, schematically based on a major and a minor triad, along with the descending tendency observed in many Brazilian folk melodies:

Example 8   "Vem cá, Bitu"

Levy's nationalism in this piece is limited to the choice of the theme, for the sixteen variations present no characteristic local elements and make no attempt to reconstruct the local atmosphere. He dedicated them to his teacher of harmony and composition, Gustav Wertheimer. Significantly, most of the variations appear as a scholastic harmonization of a given soprano part, making use of two of the main types of variation technique -- the melodic-harmonic ornamentation, and the harmonic variation. For our purpose, the only significance of this work resides in the evidence it gives of the composer's early interest in Brazilian popular musical traditions, although the means through which he expressed himself were still strongly dominated by European models.

The compositions most representative of national character were written in 1890, two years before his sudden death. They included the tone poem Comala, the Tango Brazileiro for piano, and the Suite

*   *   *

20. Cf. Francisco Augusto Pereira da Costa, "Folk-lore Pernambucano," Revista do Instituto Histórico, Vol. LXX, pt. 2, pp. 507-8. The author indicates that the Pernambuco version of "Vem cá, Bitu" is somewhat different from the song bearing the same title in Rio de Janeiro.
21. João Ribeiro, O Folklore (Rio de Janeiro: Jacintho Ribeiro dos Santos, 1919) pp. 227-9.
22. Renato Almeida, História da Música Brasileira (Rio de Janeiro, F. Briguiet & Comp. Editores, 2nd ed., 1942) p. 170.

<u>Brésilienne</u> for symphonic orchestra. Of these, only the last two will be examined here.

Published by the local newspaper <u>Diário Popular</u>, the <u>Tango Brazileiro</u> is a short piano piece whose popular appeal resulted primarily from the attempt to recreate the atmosphere of the tango. Around 1890 the tango was still very similar to the habanera. In fact, in Brazil tango was the name given to the habanera itself as well as to the "primitive adaptation of this urban dance."[23] What has not been determined is how the habanera established itself in Brazil -- whether it came from Spain (possibly via the West Indies) or through the tango from the River Plate region. According to Vicente Rossi, the habanera was also known as 'tango' in Argentina and Uruguay around the years 1889-1890.[24] The tango had the same basic rhythmic pattern as the habanera, but was slightly faster in tempo and used variants of the syncopation which also defined the general pattern of the maxixe. The tango, therefore, underwent rhythmic transformations under the influence of the maxixe to such an extent as to make it impossible to differentiate between what was then called 'Brazilian tango' and 'maxixe'. These changes are exemplified in Levy's <u>Tango</u> by variations of the basic habanera formula, ♫♫ into ♫♫♩ ♫♫♩ or ♫♩♫ already present in Callado's polkas. The introduction represents a close relationship with the maxixe, mainly because of the rhythmic drive of the melodic line:

Example 9

Although there is no quotation of folk or popular melodies, the typical sentimentality of the modinhas has inspired the thematic material. The melody of the main theme, ornamented by passing tones, échappées, and neighboring tones, contrasts with the syncopated accompaniment, by its regular rhythmic division, alternating binary and ternary divisions. As a result, the accompaniment is not subordinated to the melody:

*   *   *

23. Mário de Andrade, <u>Música, doce música</u> (São Paulo, Livraria Martins Editôra, 1963) p. 125.
24. Vicente Rossi, <u>Cosas de Negros</u> (Buenos Aires, Libreria Hachette, 1958) pp. 144-5.

Example 10

The use of the melodic minor with its characteristic ascending raised sixth and descending lowered seventh is ingeniously extended to the harmonic structure in this piece. As in the corresponding popular genre, modulations are made within neighboring keys, with constant ambiguity between the major and the minor tonic, imitating here also the prevailing modulations of the salon modinha.

Formally, the _Tango Brazileiro_ follows the structure of most urban dances: eight-bar sections with each melodic motive of four-bar length. The thematic material of the entire piece consists of two basic ideas: the melodic design of the introduction and the main theme previously quoted. Slight elaborations on these two ideas determine the various sub-sections. The following elaboration corresponds to the main theme:

Example 11

To the melodic aspect of the introduction correspond several sub-sections, 'nationally' characteristic by the rhythmic-melodic figures of the right hand, strongly reminiscent of Callado's pieces, especially the lundu "As Clarinhas e as Moreninhas:"

Example 12

The Tango Brazileiro is historically important for being the first known characteristic nationalistic work written by a professional musician. But in this direction, the Suite Brésilienne is much more significant and symptomatic of the early phase.

Levy's Suite is the forerunner of many Brazilian suites produced by later nationalist composers. This work, while conceived as a modern suite with some programmatic intention, was also intended to be a sequence of dances, as indicated by the titles of its four movements: 1. Prelúdio; 2. Dança Rústica - Canção Triste; 3. A Beira do Regato; 4. Samba. Of these, only the Prelude and the Samba fall strictly within the scope of the present study, the other two being of a general descriptive nature and therefore of marginal interest for our purpose.

The Prelude reveals the same type of writing as the fourteen Variations. The same popular tune, Vem cá, Bitu, determines the main component of the thematic material, but is never quoted in its entirety and undergoes such fundamental changes as to be sometimes barely expressed or merely suggested. The whole prelude, in fact, relies on the variation technique, but presents no rhythmic or harmonic characterization. The harmonic vocabulary and the orchestration are conventional for the period. The ninth chord is used mostly as a transitory consonance, while numerous pedal points on the tonic and dominant, as well as the usual perfect, deceptive, and plagal cadences, are found throughout. Levy's orchestra is also representative of the early romantic period, including the string quintet, harp, kettledrums (tonic and dominant), two trombones, one bass trombone, two trumpets, four horns, and the woodwinds in pair. Worthy of note is the use of the bass trombone which had been neglected in favor of the tuba since around 1830.

The last movement, Samba, can be considered as the first decisive step toward musical nationalism in Brazil. Although it remained unpublished, it was performed with great success in Rio de Janeiro in 1890 under the direction of the composer Leopoldo Miguéz and remained one of the most acclaimed pieces of the symphonic repertoire in Brazil. This enthusiastic and spontaneous reception perhaps indicates that already in 1890 the audiences of symphonic concerts were influenced by the raising popularity of the 'maxixe', the Brazilian 'tango', and the 'chôro'.

There is no doubt that a program was attached to this piece. The piano reduction made by the brother of the composer, Luiz Levy, carries the description of a dance which is assumed to be a rural samba, and gives the author's name, Julio Ribeiro. Out of context, however, this description does not specifically refer to the samba. Julio Ribeiro's novel A Carne (The Flesh), from which the quotation was extracted, was first published in 1888, and immediately became the subject of extreme controversy. As a result of the ensuing scandal, everyone in Brazil was reading A Carne.

23

There is, therefore, a strong possibility that the passage mentioned, which, in the original, refers to a samba danced on a farm, made a deep impression on Levy. Considering that Ribeiro adhered to naturalism and realism, his description of the dance -- whether or not he observed it himself directly -- was probably as objective and faithful as he could make it:

> "They danced to the sound of crude instruments. These were two big drums ('atabaques') and several square tambourines ('adufes').
>
> Squatting, holding the tall drums between their legs, straining to bend over the tops of the instruments, two old but still vigorous Africans made them sound by beating the drumheads with both hands with a violent, nervous, savage, and unrestrained rhythm.
>
> Negroes and Negresses formed a large circle, and moved about clapping their hands slowly and beating the tambourines. In the middle of the circle, a dancer jumped, whirled, crouched and leaped up, twisted his arms, contorted his neck, swung his hips, and stamped in an indescribable frenzy -- all in such a prodigality of movement, such an expenditure of muscular and nervous energy as would have tired out any white man in less than five minutes."
>
> He sang: "Serena, pomba, serená;
> Não cança de serená
> O sereno desta pomba
> Lumeia que nem metá!
> Eh! pomba! eh!"[25]

Later, Ribeiro describes the characteristic choreographic element of most Afro-Brazilian dances called 'umbigada' (from Portuguese 'umbigo' = navel), a sort of "invitation to the dance" manifested by the touching of the couple's navels. Only then does he mention specifically the samba:

> "Those who did not dance, and who did not participate in the 'samba', gathered together in a group..."[26]

The passage from Ribeiro's work is of interest not only because of its value as a contemporary account of the rural version of the samba, but also because it provides the basic program that Levy had in mind when he wrote the Samba movement of his suite. It is doubtful that the composer himself ever had the opportunity to observe a performance of this archaic type of samba. Musically, at least, he drew on quite different sources, for the

*   *   *

25. Julio Ribeiro, A Carne (Rio de Janeiro, Livraria Francisco Alves, 19th ed., 1945) pp. 104-5.
26. Ibid., p. 107.

24

samba in this movement is based on two traditional tunes well known in urban areas, "Balaio, meu bem, balaio, " already mentioned in connection with Itiberê da Cunha's <u>A Sertaneja</u>, and "Se eu te amei, " very popular in São Paulo, written by the composer José de Almeida Cabral who was chapel-master at the São Paulo Cathedral. These tunes, obviously, do not correspond to the melodic structure of the rural samba of São Paulo which, as Mário de Andrade has shown, presented a rather irregular rhythmic division.[27] In addition, it should be pointed out that the rhythm of the rural samba was rudimentary; it presented the characteristic syncopation without variation. Levy, on the other hand, remained closer to the urban dances which developed around this time and whose influence can be easily traced in this piece. The formal aspect of the <u>Samba</u>, however, is determined by the extra-musical material.

The introduction, based on a tonic pedal, presents small rhythmic units played by the bassoon which foreshadow later developments:

Example 13   (Reduction from the orchestra score)

The popular tune "Balaio, meu bem, balaio, " is first presented by oboes and clarinets, supported by the rhythmic figure outlined in the introduction. This would indicate, in the folk context, the beginning of the dance. A transitional passage in a crescendo ascending motion, based on the dotted rhythm of the main tune, leads to a variant of the theme, 'fortissimo', imitating the full participation of the chorus in the rural samba. A sudden change of atmosphere signals the appearance of the solo dancing and singing. The melodic figure played staccato by the flute imitates again the improvisation generally used in the 'choros', in which it would be performed by either flute or 'cavaquinho' (ukulele-type instrument, also of Portuguese origin). The main melody representing the solo singing is now played by oboes and clarinets. The choral answer "Eh! pomba! eh!, " performed 'fff' by brass instruments, interrupts the solo singing, thus establishing the imitation of responsorial singing practiced in the rural samba, as well as the urbanized version called 'samba de morro':

*   *   *

27. Cf. Mário de Andrade, "O Samba Rural Paulista, " in <u>Revista do Arquivo Municipal de São Paulo</u>, XLI (1937) 113.

Example 14

Reiterations of the thematic material continue, introducing rhythmic anticipations typical of the early maxixe. This time the first violins take on the rhythmic accompaniment, while the theme is assigned to oboes and clarinets. Harmonic progressions are somewhat irregular in this last passage, with modal implications as a result of the guitar-like bass progression of descending conjunct motion.

Typical of Brazilian popular music are the repeated notes of the accompaniment of the next section, anticipating the continuous flow of the accompaniment in Ernesto Nazareth's tangos. Over a C pedal played by the strings appears a new theme, derived from the popular song "Se eu te amei (Chiba)." It is quite probable, as Andrade has pointed out, that this theme was not originally written by Cabral but collected and harmonized by him, since his modinhas and lundus do not have such a melodic character.[28] By extension, the possibility that Levy knew the melody from a source other than Cabral's song should not be discarded. This theme alternates with intricate rhythmic formulas of the maxixe, the Brazilian tango, and the early urban samba.

Gradually the main theme reappears. First hinted at by the trombones, the bassoons and clarinets, and the trumpets, it is finally stated in a varied version by trumpets and clarinets. After the repetition of the first three sections, the Samba reaches its climax in an attempt to suggest the frenzy of the dance. In tutti and 'fortissimo' various elements of the basic thematic material (balaio and chiba) are combined, and the rhythms become more dynamic and intricate.

The analysis of this piece indicates above all that the popular influences which give it an unmistakable national character came from the urban environment. Rhythmically and melodically, it is closer to the Brazilian tango or polka, and to the maxixe, than to the actual folk samba.

*   *   *

28. Mário de Andrade, "Cândido Inácio da Silva e o Lundú, "in Revista Brasileira de Música, X (1944) 29-30.

Most writers have been misled by this movenent of the Suite. After the
première in Rio de Janeiro, a critic for the local newspaper A Gazeta
de Noticias wrote: "The Samba is the vivid and faithful reproduction
of the characteristic dance of the Negroes from the interior of São Paulo, in
the festivities which are disappearing nowadays..."[29] Likewise the critic
Valentim Magalhães of O Estado de São Paulo, in an overenthusiastic
comment, saw in the Samba a sort of synthesis of Brazilian music:

> "Above all, that which surprised me was the very delicate
> skill with which the maestro blended in his composition the two
> ethnic elements of Brazilian music -- the African and the
> mestizo, the 'jongo' and the 'fadinho', the sad monodic sound
> of the 'urucungo' and the 'puita', the constant echo of the
> accompaniment, and the lascivious and playful swaying move-
> ment of the 'cateretê'... at times softened by the affectation
> and the inflection of the 'lundu'. [30]

Although Levy had no great influence in the later development of
musical nationalism in Brazil -- perhaps because he was too academic a
composer -- he remains an important figure in this early movement. He
was receptive to the most characteristic elements of urban popular music,
and he was able to feel and to express at least in some degree the essential
spirit of this music. The fact that his nationalistic compositions came in
the last years of his life is noteworthy, for it shows that the nationalist
aspect of his production was not merely tentative and transitory.

*   *   *

29. Gelásio Pimenta, Alexandre Levy (São Paulo: Tip. H. Rosenbaum,
1911) p. 25.
30. Ibid., p. 24. 'Jongo' is a rural dance whose choreography recalls
that of the rural samba. 'Fadinho' is the diminutive of fado. 'Urucungo'
is a sort of rustic bass drum, 'puíta' (also 'cuíca') a friction drum.
'Cateretê' is a folk (non-dramatic) dance from the southern states.

ALBERTO NEPOMUCENO
(1864-1920)

THE DECISIVE step toward the emergence of national music in Brazil was achieved at the beginning of the twentieth century. It was then that art music in Brazil began to display a characteristic individuality. In this development the composer Alberto Nepomuceno played a role of primary importance, not only through his own works of local character but also by stimulating the creation of genuine national music.

Although Nepomuceno was born in Fortaleza, Ceará, where his father was the organist of the cathedral, he spent most of his adolescence in Recife, studying music first with his father and later with professional teachers. In 1885 he moved to Rio de Janeiro, continuing his studies while teaching piano at the Beethoven Club. His first compositions date from this period. As early as 1887 Nepomuceno showed an interest in popular music, for together with mazurkas, romances, and berceuses, his early works included a Dança de Negros, the first 'Negro dance' of the Brazilian repertoire.

A trip to Europe took him to the most celebrated music schools: Santa Cecilia in Rome, Akademische Meisterschule and Stern'schen Konservatorium in Berlin (after a stay in Vienna attending Brahms' and Hans von Bulow's concerts), and finally the Paris Conservatory where he studied organ with Guilmant. His friendship with Edvard Grieg may have had a profound influence on his resolve to create a national musical patrimony for his own country.

When Nepomuceno returned to Brazil in 1895, he had already written some compositions of national character: the String Quartet No. 3 ('Brasileiro'), the piano piece Galhofeira, and a large number of songs in the vernacular. His activities in Rio de Janeiro -- promoting the recognition of Brazilian music and composers -- are best exemplified by his campaign against the Italophile and Germanophile music critic Oscar Guanabarino, by the inclusion of works by Brazilian composers in the programs of the Association of Popular Concerts which he directed for ten years, by the restoration of some works of the late colonial composer José Mauricio Nunes Garcia, and finally by the support he gave to popular composers such as Catulo da Paixão Cearense, by the performance of their music.

In addition, Nepomuceno always revealed great interest in modern music. He was one of the first to introduce the music of Glazunov, Mussorgsky, and Debussy in Rio de Janeiro. He began a translation of Schoenberg's treatise on harmony, with the intent of having it included in the curriculum of the National Institute of Music. He also supported Villa-Lobos' incipient career by presenting his Cello Concerto in 1919 and by recommending him to the influential publisher Sampaio Araújo.[31]

*   *   *

31. Cf. "Cronologia de Alberto Nepomuceno," Jornal do Commercio (July 5 1964).

Nepomuceno's extensive production reveals his eclecticism. He wrote in practically all the traditional musical forms or genres: art songs, with Portuguese, French, Italian, Swedish, and German texts; sacred music, including a Mass and a Tantum Ergo; secular choral music, including As Uyaras, based on an Amazonic legend, with text by the folklorist Mello Morais Filho; numerous piano and organ pieces; four string quartets and a trio; operas and lyrical comedies; a symphony, several tone poems, and three suites for orchestra.[32] Of these, the Série Brasileira, the prelude O Garatuja -- both for orchestra -- the String Quartet No. 3, the piano pieces Galhofeira and Brasileira, and numerous art songs, present folk or popular material or simply draw directly upon popular music.

Nepomuceno's concern with folk and popular music is well documented in a 1917 interview published in A Epoca Theatral. Asked to discuss the characteristics of Brazilian music, the composer commented that they were to be found in those of the musics of the three basic ethnic groups that form the people of Brazil. He deplored the fact that the musical aspect of folklore had not been undertaken because folklorists lacked musical knowledge. He also revealed his awareness of several important musical traits that were later confirmed by the investigations of Mário de Andrade:

> "I have never dedicated myself to this study, but I have made, as
> an amateur, a collection of some eighty folksongs and dances,
> which I always try to increase. Almost all of these have been
> studied and classified. In this work I have verified a modality
> which is not regional, for it is found in songs collected in Pará,
> in Ceará, and in the inland of the state of Rio de Janeiro ...
> This modality, of a melodic and harmonic nature, is produced by
> the lowering of the seventh degree [leading tone] when the treble
> tends toward the sixth [submediant], as a function of the second
> or the fourth degrees. "[33]

It has been pointed out, in fact, that the minor seventh is a characteristic feature of folk and popular music in Brazil. The formula to which Nepomuceno referred ($\frac{5 - 7b - 6/4 - 5}{I - V - IV - I}$) is indeed extremely frequent. Another formula was also observed by the composer:

*   *   *

32. For complete information ref. to Sérgio Nepomuceno Alvim Corrêa, "Catálogo Geral das Obras de Alberto Nepomuceno," Revista do Livro, n26 (Sept 1964) 183-96.
33. "A Epoca Thetral entrevista o maestro Alberto Nepomuceno, " A Epoca Theatral (Dec 27 1917).

"Another characteristic modality confirmed in a great number of songs occurs when the final note is replaced by the third degree [mediant] and sometimes the fifth [dominant], or the second [supertonic], as a function of the fifth degree. In the harmonization of these songs, this gives rise to the use in the final cadences of the third and the seventh Gregorian [church] modes, respectively."[34]

Since Nepomuceno here makes the first accurate observations on the musical characteristics of Brazilian popular music, although in an academic language and for the purpose of harmonizing folk tunes, one wonders why these elements were not systematically incorporated in his own works and those of other contemporary composers. Touching on this point, the composer explained that the 'refined' European musical education adopted in Brazil -- which he himself received -- was to blame for this situation by preventing a rapprochement between art-music composers and the spirit of the folk. Still another possible explanation was that "the musical genius imbued with regionalistic sentiments, dissociating himself from all foreign influences, and therefore capable of creating a Brazilian music par excellence, " had not yet appeared.

It should be pointed out that these statements were made toward the end of the composer's life, after his most typically nationalist works had been written. Perhaps he achieved these insights and conclusions only at this late date, and thus had little opportunity to apply them in his own works. [35]

Speaking about foreign influence in the art music of Brazil, Nepomuceno was somewhat too subjective when he said:

"The formation of some types of music that are regarded by many as having a national character, such as the modinha, for example, was exclusively influenced by the Italian school, not only in regard to form, but also in regard to melodic ideas and the 'chitarrevole' [guitar-like] accompaniment."[36]

Although he strongly criticized the banality of urban popular music, he absorbed -- perhaps subconsciously -- many influences from the urban milieu of Rio de Janeiro, where he spent most of his life. It was precisely there that the national musical characteristics were most obvious.

*   *   *

34. Loc. cit.
35. An exception is mentioned in an article by Dulce Martins Lama, "Nepomuceno, sua posição nacionalista na música brasileira, " Revista Brasileira de Folclore, IV nos. 8/10 (1964) 14-15. The quotation of a letter from Nepomuceno to Baron Studart indicates the deliberate use of the lowered leading tone in his Hino ao Ceará (1903), following the model of three melodies from Ceará collected by the composer.
36. Loc. cit.

Among his first works with a nationalistic tendency was the String Quartet in D minor, No. 3, written in Europe, whose autograph was recently discovered at the library of the National School of Music of the University of Brazil. This quartet carries the designation "Brasileiro" and the manuscript bears the place and date of composition -- Berlin, 1891 -- as well as the dedication to the composer Leopoldo Miguéz, then director of that School of Music.

Conventionally treated in respect to form, the quartet is in four movements, Allegro, Andante, Intermezzo (Allegretto), and Allegretto. The Allegro presents the sonata form design somewhat altered, for each theme has a corresponding short development section. The first theme uses the rhythmic figure ♪♫, so common in urban popular music, and includes the intervals of major and diminished seventh, also characteristic of popular music. The Andante is a set of variations on an original theme which, however, recalls a traditional lullaby from the northeastern provinces, associated with the 'tutu maramba' (bogey-man) of children:

Example 15a

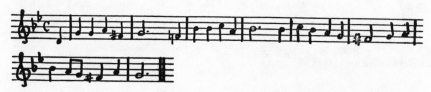

The variations are essentially melodic. In the first variation the theme is modified by extension and strictly imitated in the various parts. After the statement of the theme by the second violin, a new variation using the device of canon appears:

Example 15b

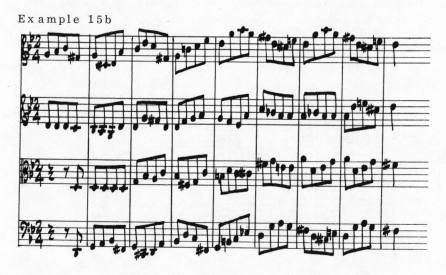

This passage anticipates to a certain extent Villa-Lobos' imitations of the 'choros' as found, for example, in the Fugue of his <u>Bachianas Brasileiras No. 1</u>. It is impossible to determine whether similar imitations here were intentional; but any Brazilian listener would easily associate this passage with the 'chôro' in which such a contrapuntal treatment is very common, giving the impression of a struggle for thematic priority among the various soloist instruments, in successive questions and answers, and in dynamic crescendo, as is the case here.

The <u>Intermezzo</u> combines the rhythmic figures ♫ and ♫, typical of the 'nationalized' polka. This movement recalls the dynamic rhythms of the 'maxixe' by the constant repetition of the same figures, and the frequency of passing tones. The last movement, monothematic, is conceived as a continuous rhythmic motion, also based on imitations. The theme bears a close relationship to that of the <u>Andante</u>, suggesting an attempt at cyclic treatment.

It is apparent that this quartet shows rather slight national characterization. Only the thematic material and the rhythmic traits pointed out draw from the local atmosphere. With such a traditional and classical genre as the string quartet Nepomuceno must have experienced a sense of limitation, for three years later in Europe when he wrote the piano piece <u>Galhofeira</u> he revealed fully his knowledge of urban popular forms.

<u>Galhofeira</u> is the last of á group of four pieces called <u>Quatro Peças Lyricas</u>, <u>Opus 13</u>. The other three pieces -- <u>Anhelo</u>, <u>Valsa</u>, and <u>Diálogo</u> -- are conventionally written within a strictly romantic style. <u>Galhofeira</u> (= jovial, merry, playful) finds in the 'maxixe' and the 'chôro' the essential elements for its descriptive intent. The entire piece is based on the syncopated accompaniment pattern found in most urban popular forms ♫♫. The structure consists simply of reiterations and variants of a descending broken-chord figure alternating with a typical melodic theme:

Example 16a

Example 16b

Elements related to most urban popular music include harmonic progressions relying for the most part on tonic and dominant functions, and modulations generally occurring within neighboring keys. The exploitation of the melodic organization of the 'maxixe' and the improvisatory aspect of the 'chôro' are to be noted here. The instrumental character of the above-mentioned thematic material makes visible this association with the 'maxixe'. The same continuous flow of the melodic design may be observed in Callado's polka Cruzes minha prima, for example, suggesting the practice of improvisation in the 'choros'. This finds its application throughout Nepomuceno's piece. Also noticeable is the accentuation of syncopations which strengthens the popular character of this piece.

        In 1897 Nepomuceno presented in a concert at the National Institute of Music his most recent symphonic works, including the Symphony in G minor, Suite Antique, As Uyaras, Epitalâmio, and the Série or Suite Brasileira. This Suite was the second, after Levy's, to appear in the repertoire of contemporary Brazilian music. But, as Luiz Heitor pointed out, Levy's suite did not have much diffusion before 1897. [37] Nepomuceno's work, therefore, revealed a promising new current, and brought him more national recognition than any of his previous compositions. Going beyond the mere use or adaptation of popular melodies and rhythms, this Suite was the first attempt to depict some typical aspects of Brazilian life. The composer did not limit his description of the Brazilian scene to a regional aspect. The first movement, Alvorada na Serra (Dawn in the Mountain), could refer only to the mountainous area of southern Brazil or that of the state of Rio de Janeiro, although it actually uses traditional material from the northeastern region. In the Intermezzo, the atmosphere of a large city such as Rio can be inferred from the allusions to the 'maxixe'. The third movement, Sesta na Rêde (Siesta in the Hammock), takes its inspiration from the composer's native state, where it was customary to take a nap during the warmest part of the day. The Batuque which forms the final movement is a sort of geographical synthesis, for the term designates all types of dances similar to the samba, so widely spread throughout many regions.

*   *   *

37. Luiz Heitor Corrêa de Azevedo, op. cit., p. 166.

In Alvorada na Serra, Nepomuceno uses a lullaby diffused throughout Brazil -- 'sapo-jururu' or 'cururu' -- which is found in almost all collections of children's songs.   This song originated from a popular 'auto' of the northeast called 'bumba-meu-boi' (an 'auto' is, in this context, a kind of dance which develops a dramatic action). [38] Characteristically the melody of this traditional tune ends on the mediant: [39]

Example 17

Sa - po cu-ru - ru   da bei-ra do rio   quan-do sa-po

gri-ta ma-ninha   diz qu'es-tá com frio

But Nepomuceno changed the final to the dominant, which is still very frequent in popular music. Over a long dominant pedal, the lullaby is quoted in its entirety, alternating between oboes and flutes. The theme does not undergo intrinsic transformations. It is repeated sequentially, with varied instrumental color, serving the purpose of a general description of the dawn, with which conventional orchestral effects are associated.

In some passages imitations of the 'sabiá' bird are noticeable.   The name 'sabiá' is applied to "any number of thrushes scattered throughout Brazil, where it is a favorite songbird."[40]   Ever since the publication in 1846 of Canção do Exílio, written in 1843 by the poet Antonio Gonçalves Dias, beginning, "Minha terra tem palmeiras, onde canta o sabiá" ("In my homeland there are palm trees, where the 'sabiá' sings"), this bird had become a symbol of the natural beauty of the Brazilian land, and for this reason Nepomuceno must have alluded to this songbird here.

The last section combines the songbird played by the flute with an outline of the 'sapo-jururu melody'. After Nepomuceno's day, this melody became widely used as a characteristic theme by most nationalistic composers.

*   *   *

38. Cf. Luiz da Câmara Cascudo, Dicionário do Folclore Brasileiro (Rio de Janeiro: Instituto Nacional do Livro, 1954) pp. 124-7.
39. Mário de Andrade has stressed and illustrated this general tendency of avoiding the tonic at the end of a phrase. Ref. to Mário de Andrade, Ensaio sôbre a música..., p. 48.
40. James L. Taylor, A Portuguese-English Dictionary (Stanford: Stanford University Press, 1958) p. 562.

The Intermezzo develops and extends the rhythmic and thematic material of the third movement of the String Quartet No. 3. Curiously enough this fact has never previously been noted, perhaps because the quartet remained unpublished. The general atmosphere of this movement is more frankly popular. According to Luiz Heitor Corrêa de Azevedo, the theme originates from "a certain maxixe very much in vogue in Rio."[41] But it has not been possible to identify this 'maxixe'. The theme is more fully developed and the characteristic rhythms more systematically employed than in the corresponding movement of the quartet. The theme undergoes the following transformation which is typical of the 'maxixe' in the restlessness of the melodic line:

Example 18

Rhythmically this section brings together the basic figures of the Brazilian 'polka', the 'tango', the 'maxixe', and the early 'samba', including the ties across bar lines or strong beats, giving the characteristic feeling of a temporary suspension of the beat:

Example 19

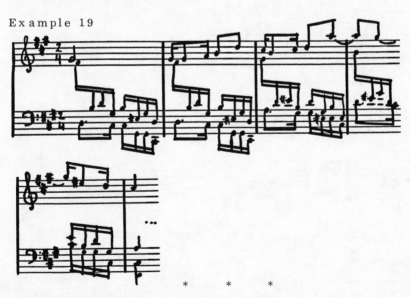

*   *   *

41. Luiz Heitor Corrêa de Azevedo, op. cit., p. 166.

Following the model of the quartet, the basic syncopation of a sixteenth, an eighth, and a sixteenth note is added to the theme in the climax -- a section which also includes the constant pattern of accompaniment by repeated notes.

The third movement (<u>Andante</u>) attempts to describe a typical Brazilian scene, without using or adapting any popular musical formula. The movement is frankly pictorial and is based on the accompanying rhythm of the strings, evoking the lazy swaying of the hammock. The basic theme, repeated throughout the piece, including the lowering of the leading tone, is also suggestive of the peaceful and monotonous atmosphere of a warm afternoon. The rocking motion is described by slow triplet figures. The local character of this piece is, however, extra-musical.

The last movement, <u>Batuque</u>, divided into two sections, is an amplified version of Nepomuceno's early piano piece, <u>Dança de Negros</u> (1887). This finale imitates the Afro-Brazilian dance by exploiting exclusively its rhythmic elements. In fact, the entire movement presents an exclusively rhythmic structure. The heavy and strongly stressed syncopations of the beginning serve as accompaniment throughout. Two syncopated melodic figures are employed as building material for the first section:

Example 20a

Example 20b

The first of these motives simulates the responsorial practice of Afro-Brazilian singing as found in 'batuques' and 'sambas', the solo part here being represented by the woodwinds and the answering chorus by strings and brass. The first part of this movement constantly reiterates this motive, except for two statements of the second figure, modulating between C major and E major in order to lessen the monotony of the repetitions. The second section

(<u>Doppio</u> <u>movimento</u>) bears the following instructions: "this movement which begins playfully ('en badinant'), becomes more and more savage toward the end." The description of the frenzy of the dance is the programmatic content of this section, which relies upon modulations, dynamics, and changes of tempo around a syncopated melodic figure repeated incessantly. Modulations alternate between F major and A-flat major. The 'savage movement' of the initial indication is rendered by a gradual acceleration of tempo and a crescendo reaching a 'furioso fortissimo', but without any alteration of the thematic figure. [42] In this <u>Batuque</u> Nepomuceno made the most of the lack of melodic characterization. The piece is indeed symptomatic of the discovery of the rhythmic primacy of popular music, prefiguring similar accomplishments in subsequent twentieth century compositions.

The <u>Suite</u> <u>Brasileira</u> represents Nepomuceno's best achievement. It is clearly indicative of this transitional period of musical nationalism in Brazil, in which conventional European procedures were combined with the incipient assimilation of popular musical forms. In addition, the <u>Suite</u> shows the composer's spontaneous awareness of, and basic interest in, the vernacular.

In 1904 Nepomuceno completed his prelude, <u>O</u> <u>Garatuja</u>, intended as the overture to a lyrical comedy based on the novel of the same name by the Indianist writer José de Alencar (1829-1877). In collaboration with Luiz de Castro, Nepomuceno wrote the complete libretto but apparently never finished the score of which only the prelude remains. [43] The novel retraces the typical customs of colonial Rio de Janeiro by creating characteristic and grotesque figures among whom is Garatuja. It is not possible to determine whether the prelude derives its material from the comedy which was to follow, but it does, nevertheless, suggest the atmosphere of the colonial city. The main theme of this piece is related to an anonymous popular 'lundu' and represents the only melodic idea which is developed in detail. Popular rhythms abound in this prelude. The typical dotted rhythm of the 'habanera' and the 'tango', and the stressed syncopations of the 'maxixe', appear throughout. Also found here are melodic designs that can be observed in the 'lundus' of the popular composer of the latter part of the nineteenth century, Xisto Bahia, as well as in the 'polkas' of Callado or F. Gonzaga, with their large skips of sevenths, octaves and ninths. By the combination of these popular elements, Nepomuceno has succeeded in giving to the prelude an unmistakable national character.

*   *   *

42. Mário de Andrade found this particular figure uncharacteristic because of its ascending motion. Although it follows the "national rhetoric," he wrote, "it does not have genuine nationality." (Cf. <u>Ensaio sôbre</u>... , p. 47.)

43. Cf. José Rodrigues Barbosa, "Alberto Nepomuceno," <u>Revista Brasileira de Música</u>, Vol. VII, pt. 1, pp. 32-3. The author states that he personally heard some passages of O Garatuja performed by the composer himself, but confesses that he does not know whether the comedy was completed or not.

One of the composer's last works was the piano piece B r a s i l e i r a, composed in 1919, in which influences of urban popular music are more clearly evident than in any other composition.   Especially notable is the similarity with Ernesto Nazareth's 'tangos' which are also highly sophisticated.

Supported by the same type of broken-chord or arpeggio accompaniment as appears in many of Nazareth's pieces, the melodic line of B r a s i l e i r a draws closer to popular music in its syncopated rhythm ♪♫|♫♫ and its harmonic implications:

Example 21

The frequent use of parallelism in connection with triads, (omitting the root), as well as ordinary seventh chords, (omitting the third or the fifth), is one of the most prominent harmonic features of Brazilian popular music. It is found in almost all of Nazareth's tangos, among which R a m i r i n h o offers the most systematic example:

Example 22a   Nazareth's R a m i r i n h o

Example 22b   Nepomuceno's <u>Brasileira</u> (middle section)

Rhythmically, <u>Brasileira</u> is very close to the popular 'maxixe' of the early twentieth century. The syncopations of the 'tango-habanera' and the 'maxixe' are alternated here with triplets, recalling once more Nazareth's 'tangos'.

Although some results had been achieved during the latter part of the nineteenty century in encouraging the use of the vernacular in the operatic repertoire, especially through the efforts of Francisco Manuel da Silva composer of the national anthem and through the founding of the Imperial Academy of Music and National Opera in 1857, art songs made use of French, Italian, and German texts, being in nowise distinguishable from the standard romantic art song literature. One exception was, of course, the early 'modinha' as an art form. Nepomuceno himself followed the general practice during his early years, in his songs with French, Italian, Swedish, and German texts, dating from the late 1880s and early 1890s. Later his nationalist orientation may have led him to use the vernacular in his songs. Indeed, in terms of musical nationalism, the close relationship between music and poetry advocated by romantic composers and continued by nationalist composers had as its natural consequence the use of the vernacular. In this respect, it is quite probable that the example of Grieg's songs with Norwegian texts may have stimulated Nepomuceno, for his sojourn at Bergen occurred in 1893, and his first songs in the vernacular date from 1894, while he was in Paris.

As soon as Nepomuceno returned to Brazil, he attempted to introduce the vernacular for singing in the concert hall, using in this campaign his well-known motto: "The people who do not sing in their own language do not have a fatherland. " ("Não tem pátria o povo que não canta na sua língua. ") This campaign was mainly directed against the long-established preconception that Brazilian Portuguese was inadequate for artistic singing. [44]   Nepomuceno eventually succeeded in his endeavors, and use of the vernacular in singing became compulsory at the National Institute of Music.

*   *   *

44. <u>Ibid.</u>, p. 25.

Within Nepomuceno's total vocal production we find some fifty songs
with Portuguese texts. With the exception of a translation from Rabindranath
Tagore, the texts were drawn from celebrated Brazilian romantic, parnassian,
and symbolist poets, such as Gonçalves Dias, Machado de Assis, Olavo Bilac,
Raimundo Correia, and lesser figures like Fontoura Xavier and Osório Duque
Estrada. Special mention should be made of the poet Juvenal Galeno (1836-
1931), who created and cultivated popular poetry based on the folkways of his
native state of Ceará. The national character of Nepomuceno's songs has
generally been somewhat overestimated. While the 'modinha' and the 'lundu'
appear to have exerted considerable influence on the composer, the national
traits of the songs remain limited. Coração Triste (Op. 18 No. 1),
for example, on Machado de Assis' poem, recalls the simplicity of the
melodic line of the 'modinha', but does not otherwise present a well-defined
national character. On the other hand, he tried to avoid the attraction of
the picturesque which lured many of his epigoni.[45] In so doing, he deliberately
limited direct quotations and imitations of popular and folk music. His concern
with national sources is more evident in the choice of poetic texts than in the
music itself. The song Numa Concha, for example, to verses by Olavo
Bilac, presents an uncharacteristic melody, although the accompaniment
exhibits the usual syncopations of popular guitar players.

Xácara (Op. 20 No. 1) is considered by many as one of the best of
Nepomuceno's vocal works. The song is directly inspired by the 'modinha'
of the Second Empire in the vocal line, and by the popular 'modinha' in the
accompaniment. The melody recalls the 'modinha' by its repeated notes
and small intervals. The accompaniment repeats the same syncopated
figure, softened by a triplet, imitating the guitaresque fingering.

Some errors of accentuation, diphthongs, or union of words have been
pointed out in Nepomuceno's songs.[46] Although hiatus and synalepha follow
generally the spoken language, Nepomuceno seems to be too much constrained
by respect for the beat. Often the rhythmic division of the vocal line does not
correspond to the prosodic caesura.

A Jangada (1920) was the last composition of Nepomuceno. The
poem, from Galeno's collection Lendas e Canções Populares (1865),
describes the typical raft ('jangada'), a sort of catamaran, used by fishermen
off the coast of the northeastern states. This song is perhaps the most
nationalist of all, mainly because of its rhythmic and harmonic elements,

*   *   *

45. Cf. Andrade Muricy, "O Lied brasileiro nasceu com Alberto
Nepomuceno, " Jornal do Commercio (Aug 30 1939).
46. Mário de Andrade, "Os Compositores e a Língua Nacional, "
Anais do Primeiro Congresso da Língua Nacional Cantada, (São
Paulo, 1938) p. 124.

including the basic syncopations of the accompaniment, harmonic progressions imitating the guitar-like accompaniments in descending motion by conjunct degrees, repeated notes, and the descending tendency of the vocal line.

In spite of the expressive qualities of his songs, one has to recognize that the fundamental significance of Nepomuceno as a song composer lies in the diffusion of the vernacular rather than in the creation of genuine Brazilian art-songs. In this respect, he stands as a pioneer, opening the path to subsequent nationalist song composers.

Alberto Nepomuceno has been proclaimed as the "father of Brazilian music" by the composer Camargo Guarnieri, and the "founder of Brazilian music" by Rodrigues Barbosa and other writers. The exaggeration of these epithets is obvious, for Nepomuceno was not an exception among the romantic composers of the late nineteenth and early twentieth centuries in Brazil. He did not escape the overwhelming domination of European music. He was not the founder of anything, but he was attentive to his own environment, so that the popular influences in his nationalistic compositions constitute an integral part of their style.

––––––––––––––––

THE EFFECTS of popular music on the national art music of the period considered here have proved particularly crucial. Among the various factors which contributed to the development of these popular musical currents, the dynamism of urban life after the proclamation of the Republic -- which determined the rapprochement of folksongs and dances with imported urban dances -- was very important. Popular composers such as Joaquim A. Callado, Francisca Gonzaga, Ernesto Nazareth, and others represented to a certain extent the link between folk traditions and the highly sophisticated urban music saturated with imported elements. They can be considered responsible for the nationalization of European dances and for the popularization of more traditional forms such as the 'modinha' and the 'lundu'. Furthermore, these composers introduced the new popular species of the 'tango', the 'maxixe', and the early urban 'samba', from which the vernacular music emerged.

41

The principal musical characteristics of these species are undoubtedly found in the fundamentally rhythmic nature of most Afro-Brazilian dances which is revealed by syncopation. The systematic employment of the syncopation of a sixteenth, eighth, and sixteenth notes, peculiar to all Afro-American music, is found in all the new types of popular music which appeared during the period 1880-1920. Likewise the syncopated accent is conspicuous in almost all of the art compositions examined in this study. But while the art composers of the early nationalist period made systematic use of syncopation, they generally limited it to the figures of the 'tango' and the 'habanera', or to the syncopation accent, thus remaining unaware of the rhythmic anticipations and the "offbeat phrasing of melodic accents"[47] that the contemporary popular composers, basing their practice on Brazilian prosody, frequently employed.

The melodic aspect of the new types of popular music also enhanced this phase of rhythmic predominance. In this respect an analysis of Nazareth's 'tangos' shows the strictly instrumental character of the melodic line, favoring its rhythmic transformation. Aside from the passages where 'modinha' influences have been noted, the most characteristically 'national' art compositions studied here have demonstrated the same tendency, the most convincing examples being Levy's Samba from the Suite Brésilienne, and Nepomuceno's Batuque from the Série Brasileira. Furthermore, the descending melodic motion that can be observed in popular music also characterizes most of the nationalistic art compositions, with the exceptions mentioned. Finally, the 'serenading' aspect of the choros which later influenced Heitor Villa-Lobos introduced to urban popular music of this period the improvisatory peculiarity of the melodic phrases, revealing a fluctuating and unsymmetrical progression. This peculiarity, which distinguishes the works of Callado, Gonzaga, and above all Nazareth, has been noticed often in Levy's Tango Brazileiro and Samba, and in Nepomuceno's Galhofeira and Brasileira.

Harmonically, the period under consideration had no distinctive character that sets it apart from European types of harmonization. Certain common harmonic formulas found in the 'modinha' could be identified with Brazilian 'national' music only by reason of their frequent use. Likewise the imitation of guitar-like accompaniments brought about frequent

*   *   *

47. Richard Alan Waterman, "African Influence on the Music of the Americas," in Proceedings of the 29th International Congress of Americanists, II (Chicago, 1952) 212. Syncopation "in terms of total musical effect," when applied to African or Afro-American music in general, "is felt to be misleading" by the author, who prefers the quoted designation on the ground that there exists a "rhythmic awareness" but not a metronomic beat in which all accents would occur.

parallelism in connection with triads or seventh chords, and accentuation of the conjunctly moving bass.

Thus the popular elements that have been identified in the art compositions were basically of a melodic and rhythmic nature. These elements were taken mostly from urban popular music, since most art-music composers remained unaware of the primary forms of folk music. Folksongs and dances were known indirectly through their transformation into the new urban popular forms.

No absolute answer can be given to the question of how this urban popular music affected the art music of the period. It is apparent that the popular composers mentioned here -- who contributed in such a high degree to the emergence of the new types of popular music -- had no direct influence on the first nationalist composers. They prepared, however, a suitable musical environment, deeply rooted in popular traditions and therefore favorable to the emergence of nationalism.

While it must be admitted that both Levy and Nepomuceno were strongly stimulated by European nationalistic movements, it is also evident that they recognized the value of Brazilian urban popular music in general as a source to which they could most naturally turn. In so doing, however, they assimilated only its extrinsic peculiarities. It was left to composers of succeeding generations -- from Gallet and Villa-Lobos to Guarnieri and Santoro -- to create nationalistic works in a freer style, without being so closely bound to popular musical sources.